SUGAR AND SPICE

RHYTHMS AND TUNES FOR BEGINNERS

LELA HOOVER WARD

Illustrations by Ruth Ward Farrell

Copyright, 1948, by THE BOSTON MUSIC CO.
International Copyright Secured

The Boston Music Co., Boston, Mass.

Copyright, 1948, by The Boston Music Co.
International Copyright Secured

FOREWORD

In music, rhythm is of prime importance, and should be taught first by clapping the hands and counting. In this book the music has been kept simple so that basic time may be observed.

The pieces have been written and arranged to allow normal hand position, and to encourage correct fingering. Finger Fun is tuneful, and should be played slowly and steadily, with good hand and finger position, counting aloud.

It has been left to the discretion of the teacher when to give the pupil the names of the note values—semibreve, minim, crotchet and quaver.

RHYTHMS

$\frac{2}{4}$ $\frac{3}{4}$ $\frac{4}{4}$ using semibreves, minims and crotchets

$\frac{2}{4}$ $\frac{3}{4}$ $\frac{4}{4}$ introducing quavers

$\frac{2}{4}$ $\frac{3}{4}$ $\frac{4}{4}$ introducing triplets

$\frac{2}{4}$ $\frac{3}{4}$ $\frac{4}{4}$ introducing dotted crotchets

---

CONTENTS

COOKIE MAN 4	MY BLACK HEN ...... *Mother Goose* 17
MY RED DRUM 5	AIR FROM BACH ...... *Chorale* 18
THE MULBERRY BUSH .... *English Singing Game* 6	COURT DANCE 19
IN THE SWING 7	BY THE RIVER 20
MY GOOD FRIEND PIERROT .. *French Folk Song* ... 8	MARCH TIME 21
WEE WILLIE WINKIE .... *Nursery Rhyme* 9	RUSSIAN DANCE 22
A SCOTTISH DANCE 10-11	LONDON BRIDGE .... *English Singing Game* 23
A LITTLE WALTZ 12	BLOW THE MAN DOWN .... *Sea Chantey* 24
'ROUND AND 'ROUND 13	SILENT NIGHT .... *Gruber* 25
NODDING DAISIES 14	ALL THROUGH THE NIGHT .. *Old Welsh Air* 26
TEN LITTLE INDIANS 15	SLUMBER SONG .... *Schubert* 27
THE BUGLER 16	

For Billy and Ward Morrison

Cookie Man

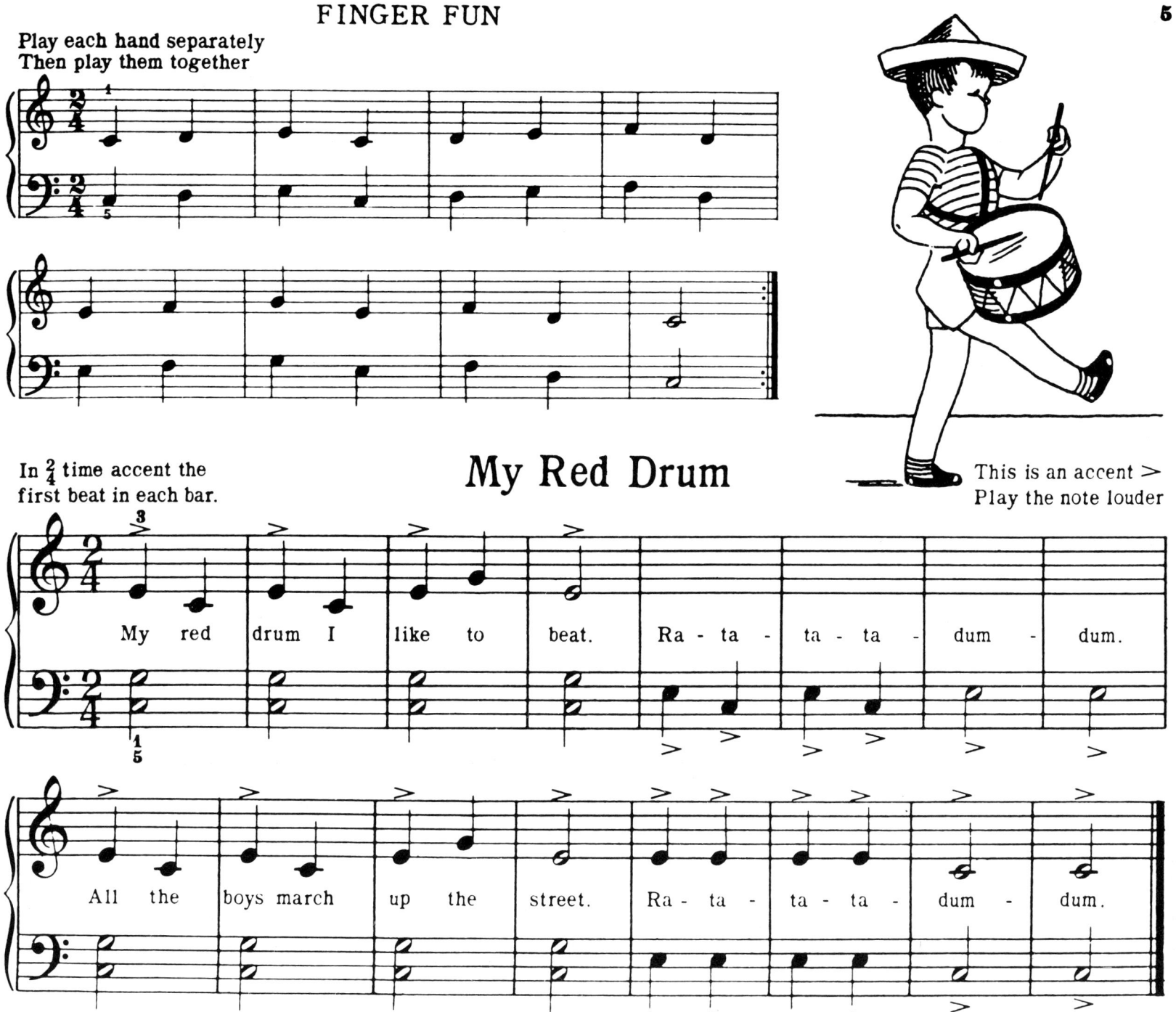

Give 𝅗𝅥. three beats
This is an accent >

The Mulberry Bush

In 3/4 time accent the
first beat in each bar

English Singing Game

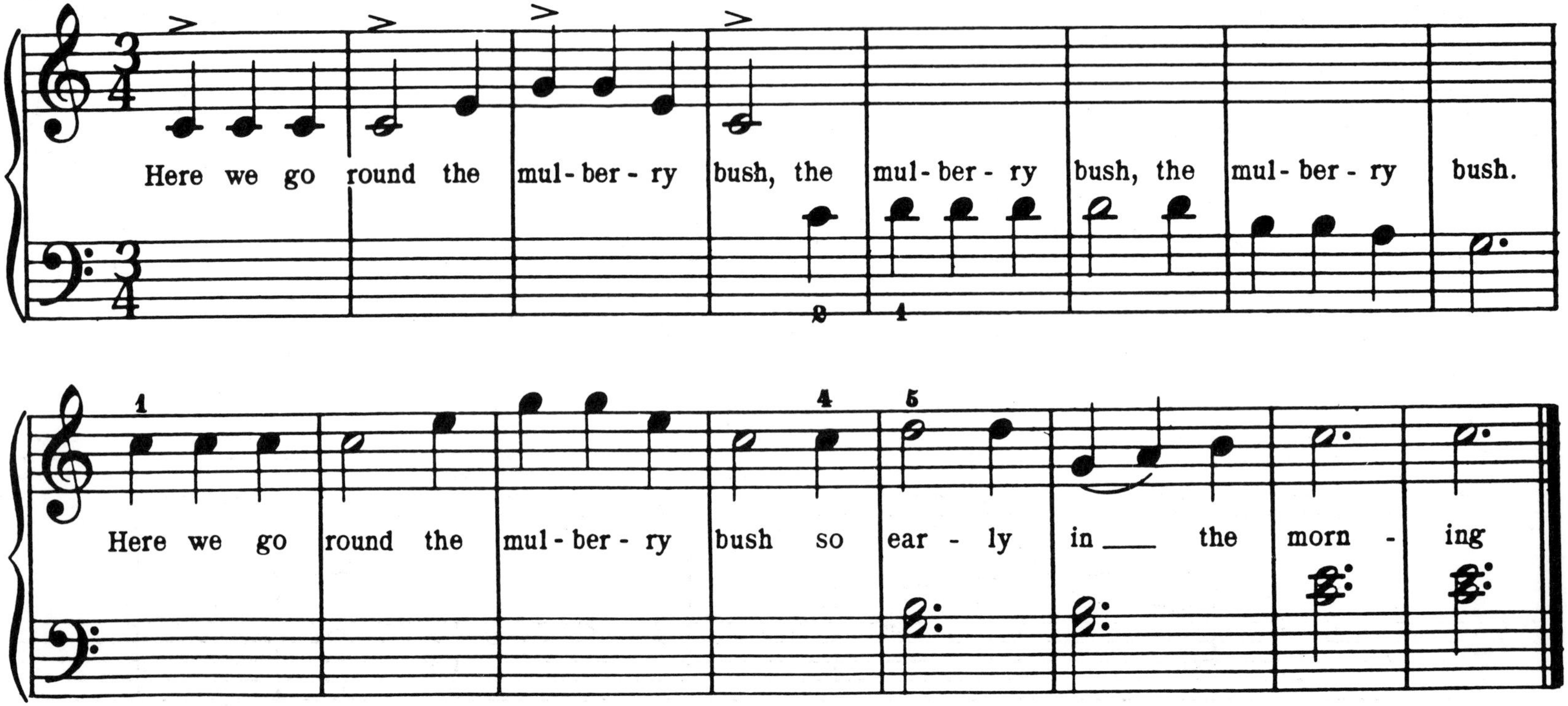

Here we go round the mul-ber-ry bush, the mul-ber-ry bush, the mul-ber-ry bush.

Here we go round the mul-ber-ry bush so ear-ly in the morn-ing

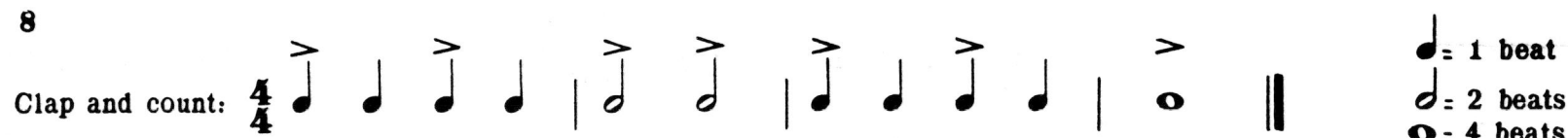

FINGER FUN

In 4/4 time accent the first and third beat in each bar

My Good Friend Pierrot

French Folk Song

Now the moon is shin-ing, my good friend Pier-rot; Wa-ken from thy slum-ber hear me knock-ing low.
I must write a let-ter: lend your pen, I pray. Dead now is my can-dle, gone the light of day.

Clap and count:

say: one two - oo one two - oo wa - un two - oo one two

 These notes go in pairs

 = 1 beat

A Scottish Dance

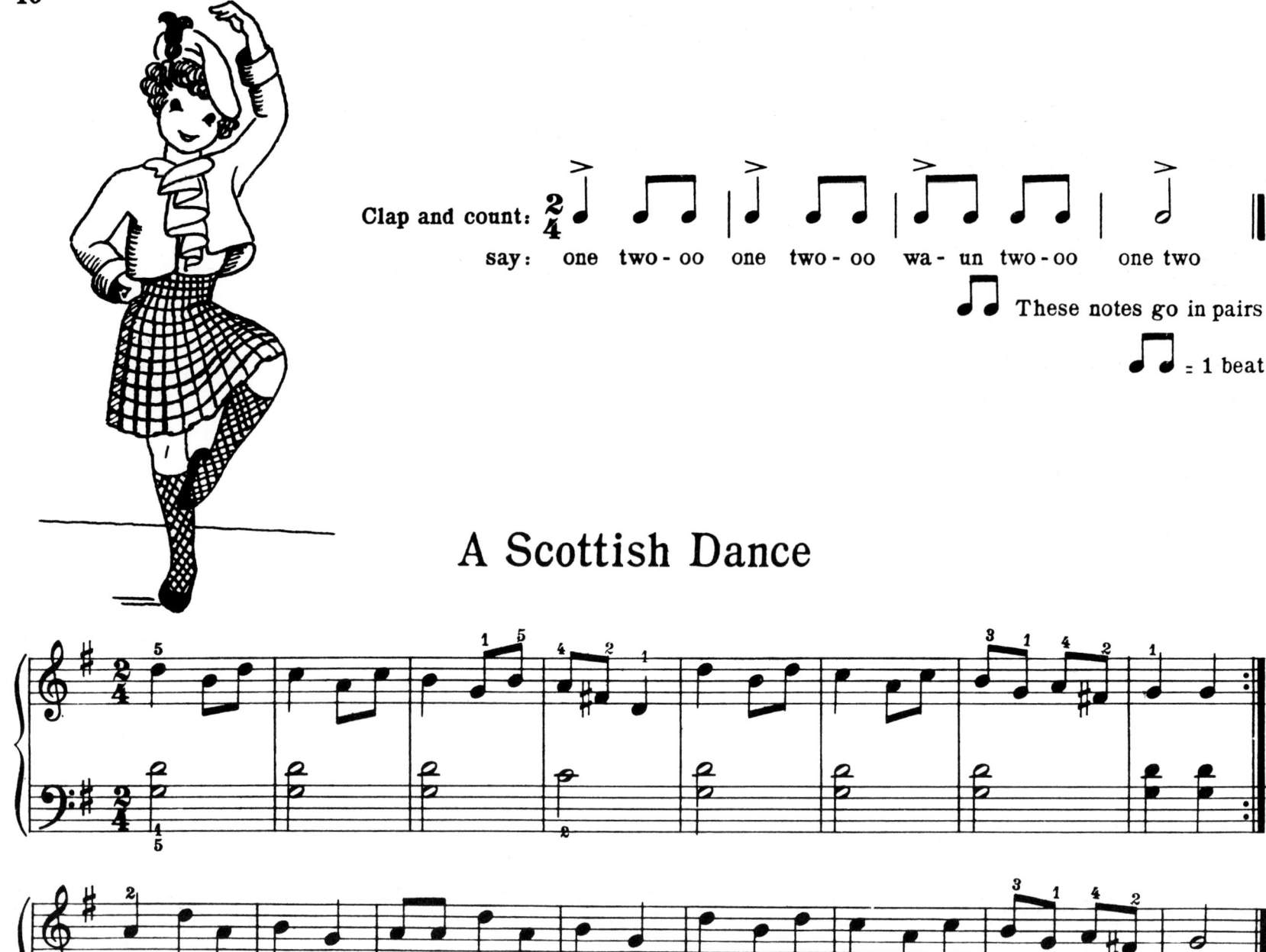

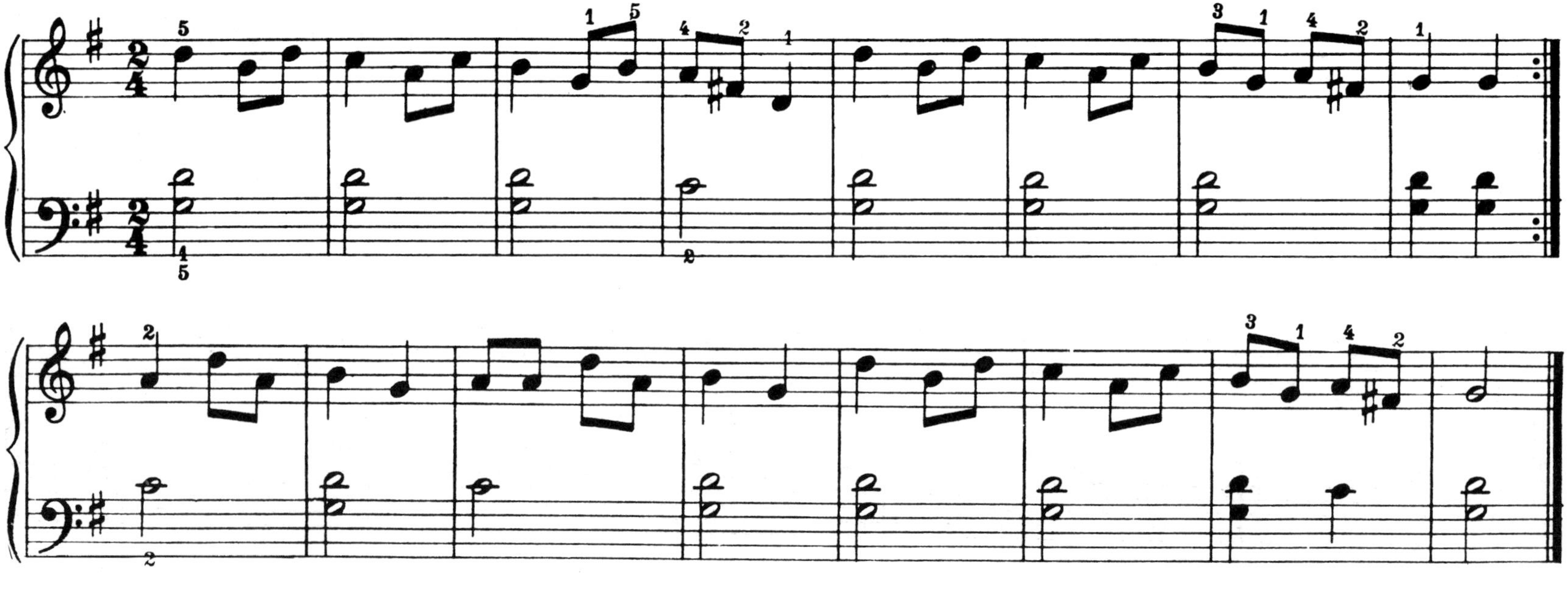

FINGER FUN

Sometimes these pairs ♫
go by themselves, like this: ♪♪

Play the Scottish Dance again.
It looks different, but it sounds
the same.

A Scottish Dance

Clap and count:

say: wa - un two - oo three - ee 1 2 3 wa - un two - oo three - ee 1 2 3

This is a 1 beat rest -

This dot means cut the note short -

This is called staccato

Right hand staccato
Make left hand sing

A Little Waltz

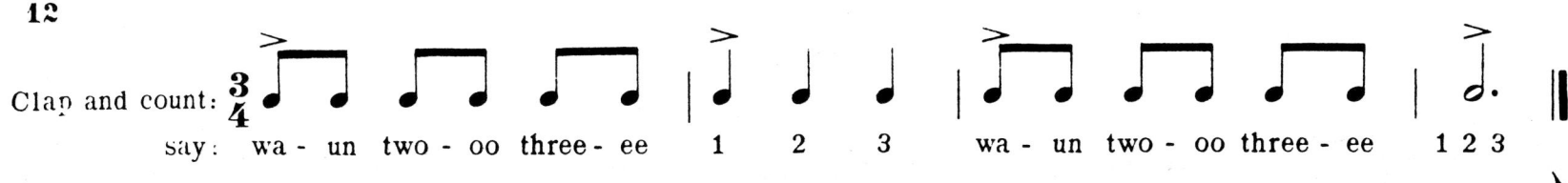

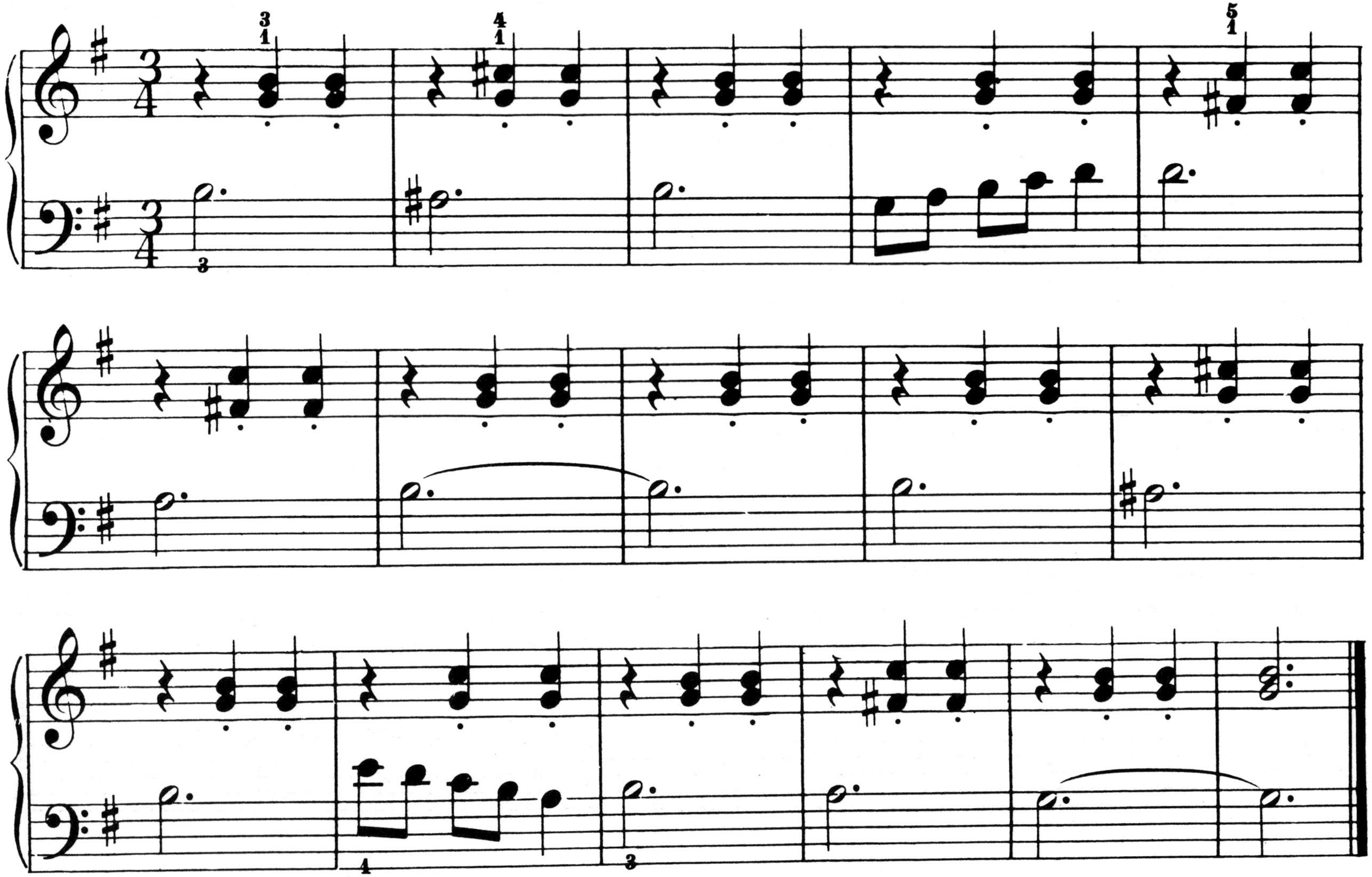

FINGER FUN

'Round and 'Round

Remember to accent

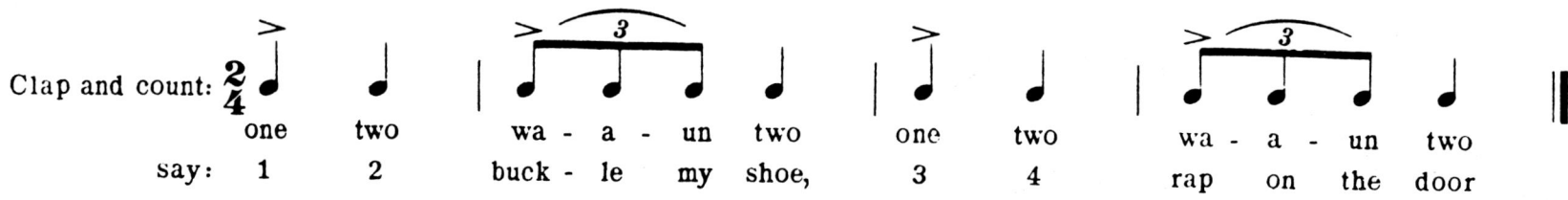

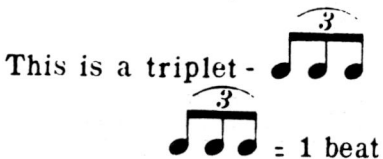

The Bugler

Drums

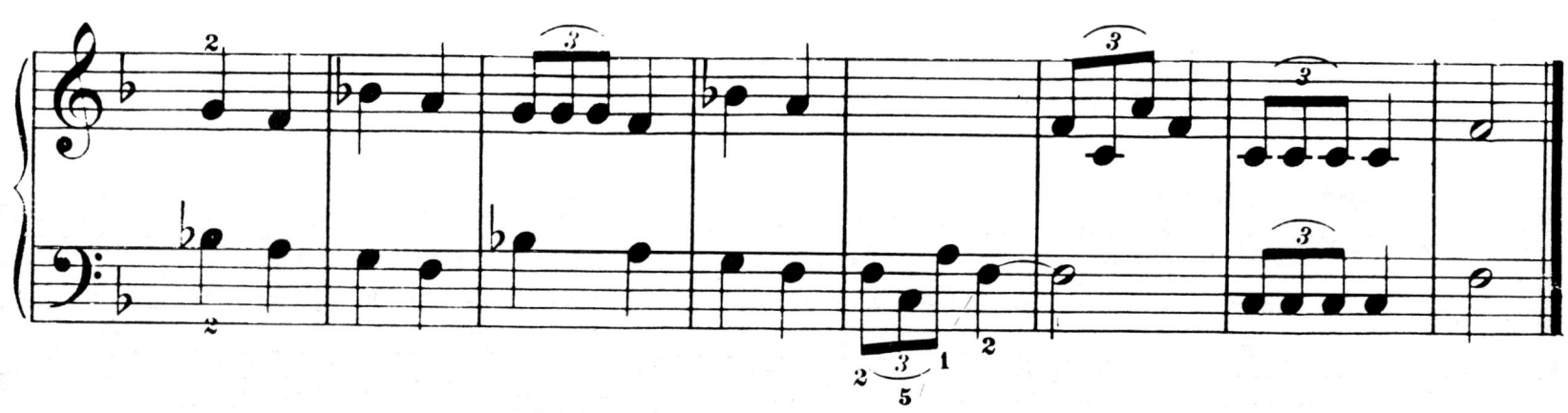

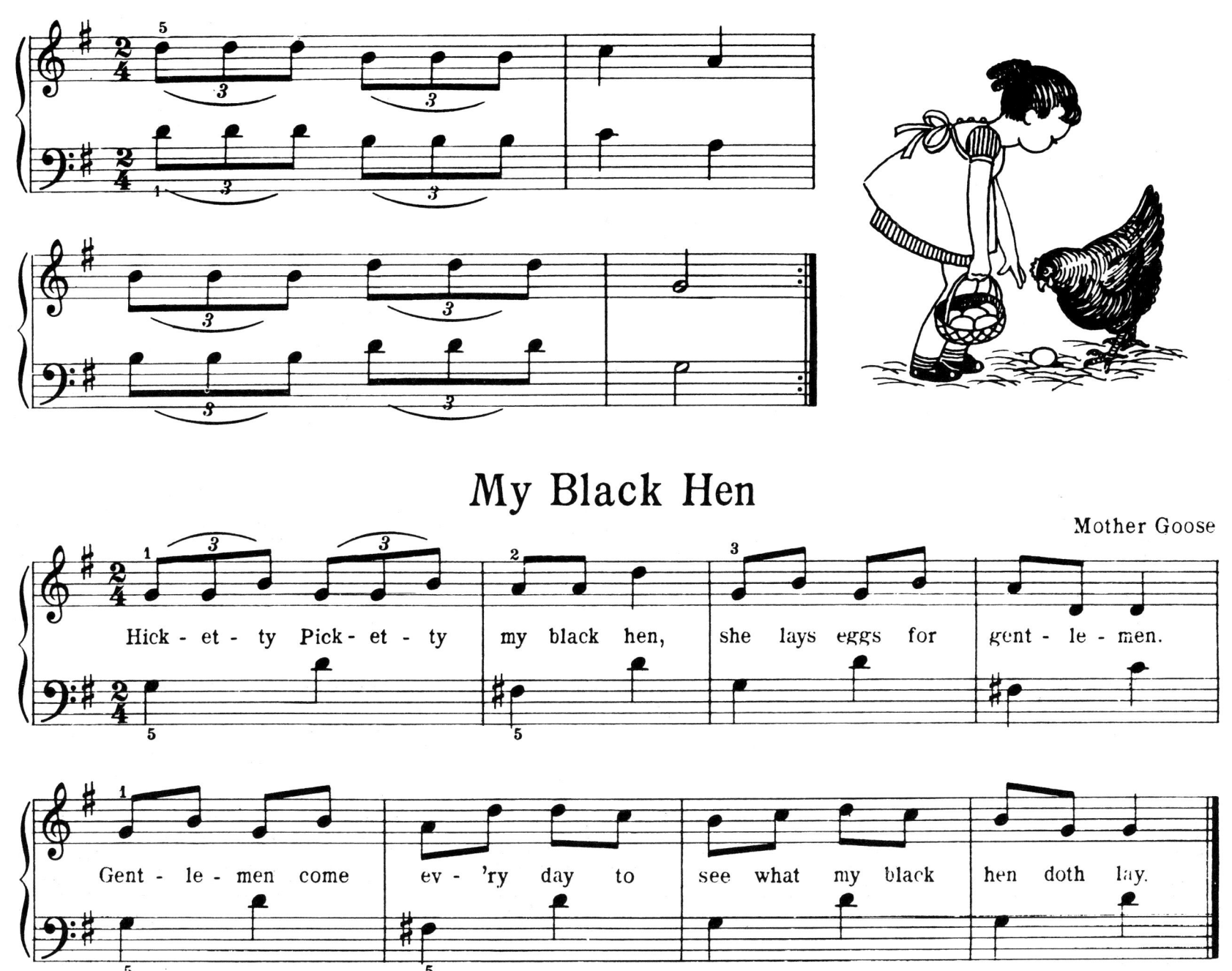

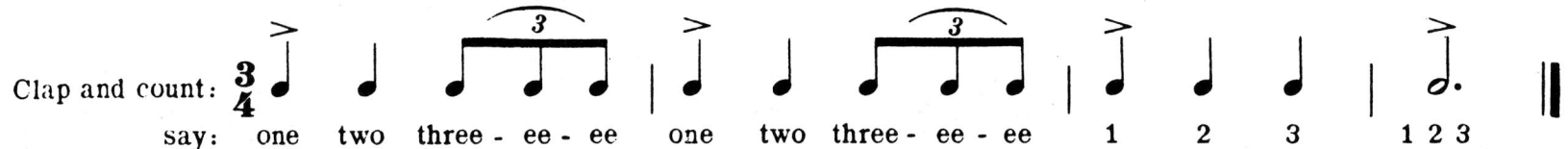

Air from Bach

Chorale

FINGER FUN

Court Dance

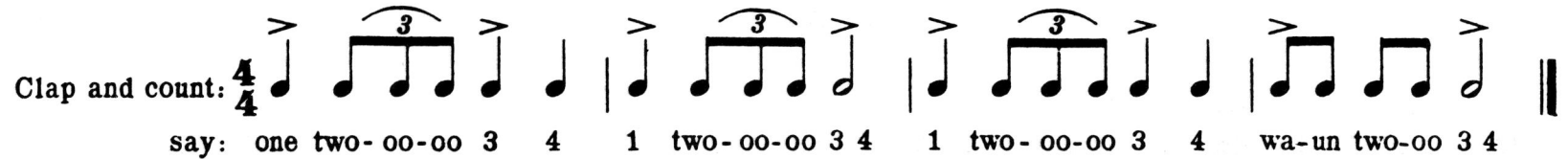

By the River

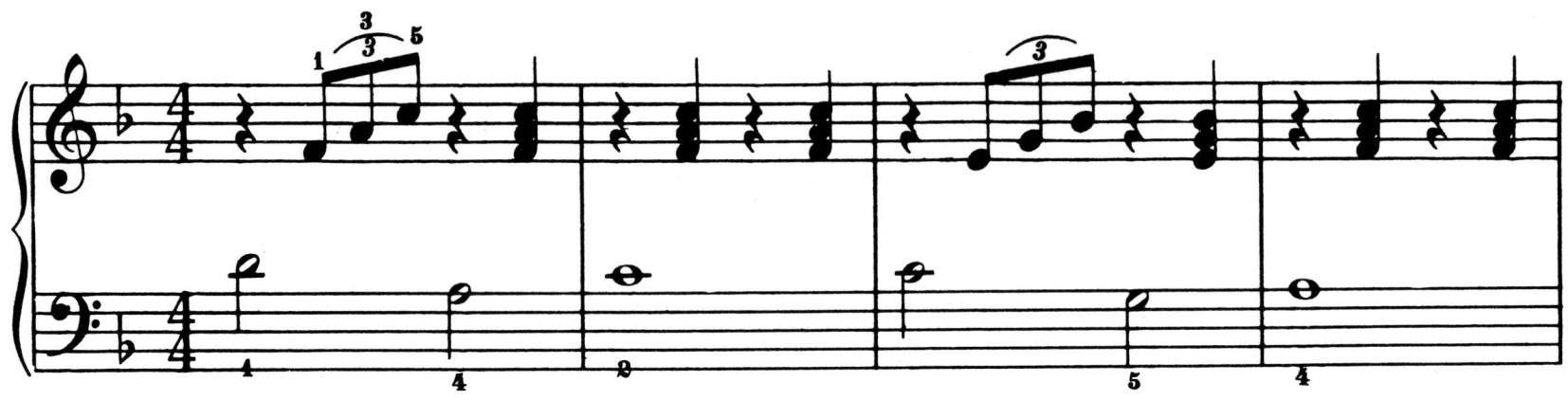

FINGER FUN

This is a 4 beat rest

March Time

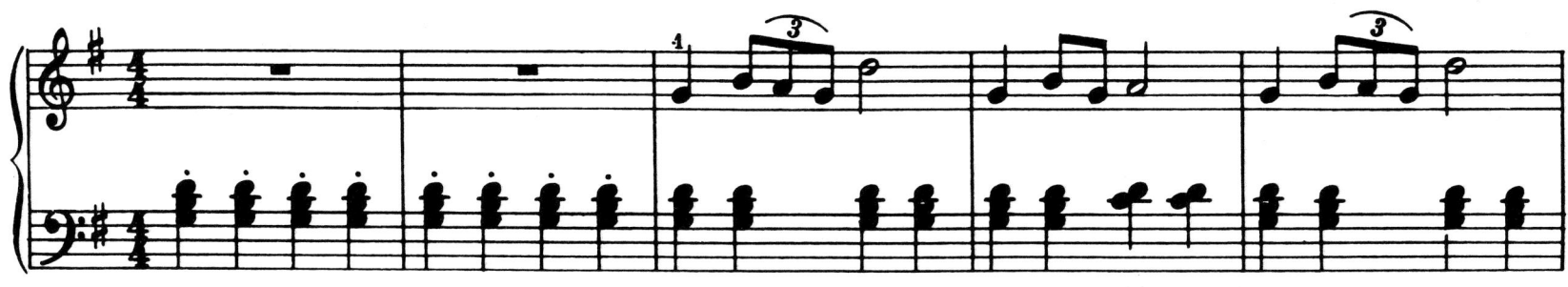

FINGER FUN

London Bridge

English Singing Game

Blow the Man Down

Sea Chantey

Silent Night

Franz Gruber

Clap and count:

All Through the Night

L. W. D.

Old Welsh Air

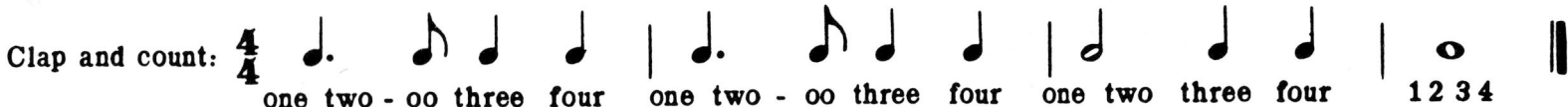

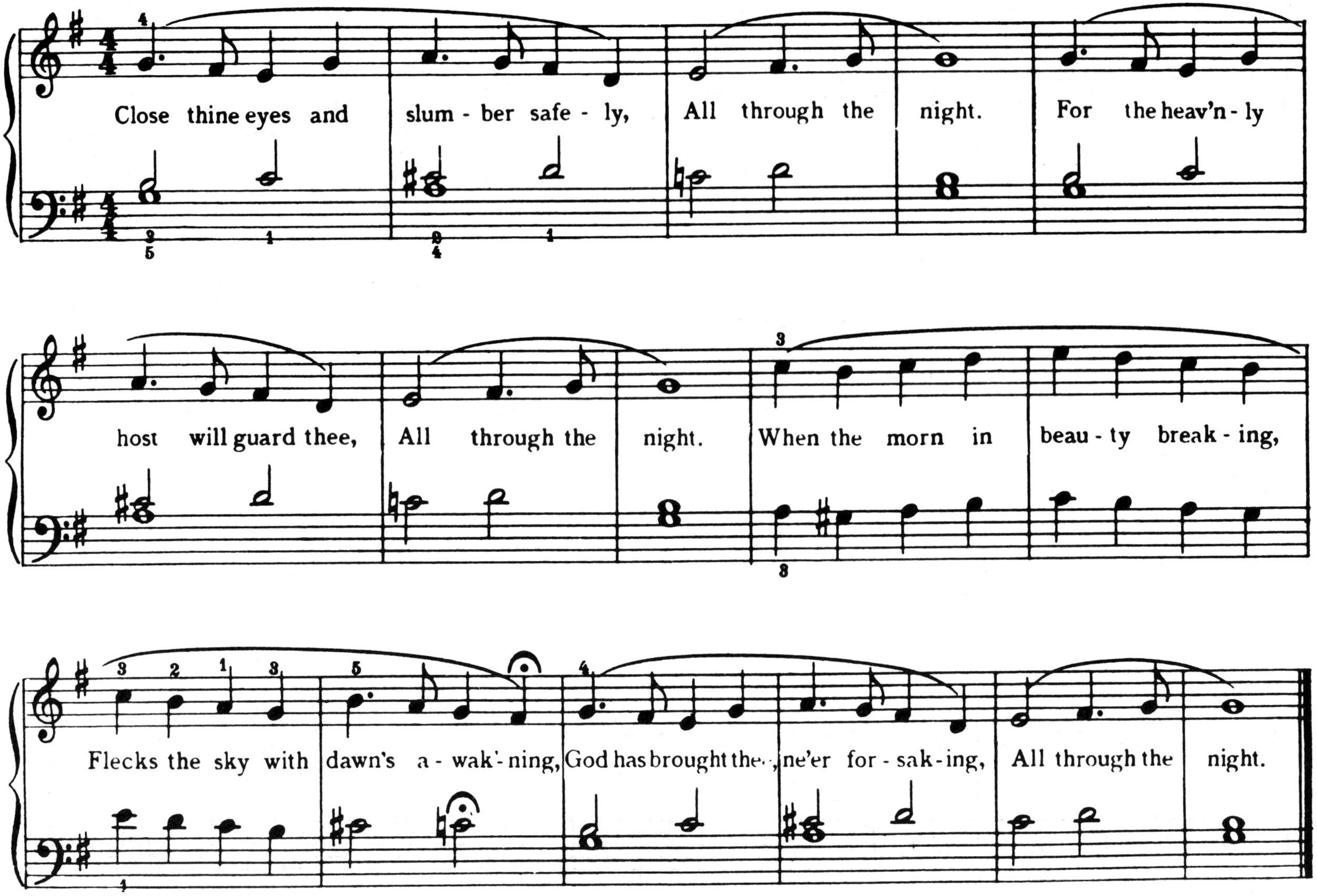